MUCIZE MISAFIR MERHABA

Abhijit Naskar is the 21st century Neuroscientist and Poet who has been serving at the forefront of humankind's struggle against sectarianism. As an untiring advocate of mental health and global harmony, he became a beloved best-selling author across the world with his very first book "The Art of Neuroscience in Everything". With his revolutionary contributions in Cognitive and Behavioral Neuroscience Naskar has helped the world tackle the horrors of systemic racism, biases, hate, extremism, discrimination and stereotypes more effectively, because of which he is lovingly hailed by humankind as 'the humanitarian scientist'.

Mucize Misafir
Merhaba

The Peace Testament

ABHIJIT NASKAR

Also by Abhijit Naskar

The Art of Neuroscience in Everything
Your Own Neuron: A Tour of Your Psychic Brain
The God Parasite: Revelation of Neuroscience
The Spirituality Engine
Love Sutra: The Neuroscientific Manual of Love
Homo: A Brief History of Consciousness
Neurosutra: The Abhijit Naskar Collection
Autobiography of God: Biopsy of A Cognitive Reality
Biopsy of Religions: Neuroanalysis towards Universal
Tolerance
Prescription: Treating India's Soul
What is Mind?
In Search of Divinity: Journey to The Kingdom of Conscience
Love, God & Neurons: Memoir of a scientist who found
himself by getting lost
The Islamophobic Civilization: Voyage of Acceptance
Neurons of Jesus: Mind of A Teacher, Spouse & Thinker
Neurons, Oxygen & Nanak
The Education Decree
Principia Humanitas
The Krishna Cancer
Rowdy Buddha: The First Sapiens
We Are All Black: A Treatise on Racism
The Bengal Tigress: A Treatise on Gender Equality
Either Civilized or Phobic: A Treatise on Homosexuality
Wise Mating: A Treatise on Monogamy
Illusion of Religion: A Treatise on Religious
Fundamentalism
The Film Testament
Human Making is Our Mission: A Treatise on Parenting
I Am The Thread: My Mission
7 Billion Gods: Humans Above All
Lord is My Sheep: Gospel of Human
Morality Absolute
A Push in Perception
Let The Poor Be Your God
Conscience over Nonsense
Saint of The Sapiens
Time to Save Medicine
Fabric of Humanity
Build Bridges not Walls: In the name of Americana
The Constitution of The United Peoples of Earth

Lives to Serve Before I Sleep
When Humans Unite: Making A World Without Borders
All For Acceptance
Monk Meets World
Mission Reality
Citizens of Peace: Beyond The Savagery of Sovereignty
Operation Justice: To Make A Society That Needs No Law
See No Gender
The Gospel of Technology
Every Generation Needs Caretakers: The Gospel of
Patriotism
Aşkanjali: The Sufi Sermon
Mad About Humans: World Maker's Almanac
Revolution Indomable
When Call The People: My World My Responsibility
No Foreigner Only Family
Hurricane Humans: Give me accountability, I'll give you
peace
Ain't Enough to Look Human
Servitude is Sanctitude
Time To End Democracy: The Meritocratic Manifesto
I Vicdansaadet Speaking: No Rest Till The World is Lifted
Boldly Comes Justice: Sentient not Silent
Good Scientist: When Science and Service Combine
Sleepless for Society
Neden Türk: The Gospel of Secularism
Martyr Meets World: To Solve The Hard Problem of
Inhumanity
The Shape of A Human: Our America Their America
When Veins Ignite: Either Integration or Degradation
Heart Force One: Need No Gun to Defend Society
Solo Standing on Guard: Life Before Law
Generation Corazon: Nationalism is Terrorism
Mucize Insan: When The World is Family
Hometown Human: To Live for Soil and Society
Girl Over God: The Novel (Abi Naskar Adventures Book 1)
Gente Mente Adelante: Prejudice Conquered is World
Conquered
Earthquakin' Egalitarian: I Die Everyday So Your Children
Can Live
Giants in Jeans: 100 Sonnets of United Earth
Vatican Virus: The Forbidden Fiction (Abi Naskar
Adventures Book 2)
Karadeniz Chronicle: The Novel (Abi Naskar Adventures

Book 3)
Şehit Sevda Society: Even in Death I Shall Live
Handcrafted Humanity: 100 Sonnets For A Blunderful
World
Mücadele Muhabbet: Gospel of An Unarmed Soldier
Making Britain Civilized: How to Gain Readmission to The
Human Race
Dervish Advaitam: Gospel of Sacred Feminines and Holy
Fathers
Honor He Wrote: 100 Sonnets For Humans Not Vegetables
The Gentalist: There's No Social Work, Only Family Work
Either Reformist or Terrorist: If You Are Terror I Am Your
Grandfather
Woman Over World: The Novel (Abi Naskar Adventures
Book 4)
High Voltage Habib: Gospel of Undoctrination
Bulldozer on Duty
Find A Cause Outside Yourself: Sermon of Sustainability
Ingan Impossible: Handbook of Hatebusting
Amor Apocalypse: Canım Sana İhtiyacım
Amantes Assemble: 100 Sonnets of Servant Sultans

DEDICATION

This book is dedicated to the impossible peacemaker.

CONTENTS

1. Mind Makes The World

What is the enemy of knowledge? Some may say ignorance, which may be correct to some extent. But there is something far worse than ignorance.

You know what is worse than ignorance?

It's half knowledge.

Half knowledge is more dangerous than ignorance. Take the notion that jellyfish don't have a brain, for example. When we talk about the brain, we're actually referring to the central nervous system. In case of the jellyfish, the nervous system is not centralized, instead it's spread across the anatomy.

So the actual fact is, jellyfish do have a brain, it just doesn't look like one. Even trees have a brain, a nervous system that is. To put it simply, consciousness is the supreme fundamental of life, and it is impossible to have consciousness without having some sort of nervous system, for consciousness is the creation of the nervous system.

Brain makes the mind, mind makes the person. And that brain holds both the heart and the head that we often rhetorically talk about, while the physical heart only pumps blood.

Yet many still believe that the physical heart is the actual source of our emotions.

That is why I say, save love, question everything. Question every single belief and opinion that you come across in life, both inside and outside – not out of condescension or intellectualism, but out of plain curiosity.

Remember this. Every time I have something to say, I ask myself three questions - is it right, is it necessary, is it human!

2. Question The Ism

You may wonder, why is it of such great importance that we question everything! So let me elaborate a bit further. Take the jellyfish matter for example. The notion of jellyfish not having brain helps sustain the prehistoric superstition that consciousness comes from an external supernatural source.

Now the point is, I got no problem if the civilians are not aware of the rudimentary facts of brain and consciousness, for the purpose of belief is not to acquaint us with truth, but ensure self-preservation. However, any belief that dissociates the mind from accountability is not only detrimental to that individual, but also to the entire society.

Now let's take a step further. If the civilians of the world had the common sense to question nationalism for example, all wars would've disappeared long ago.

What do they do instead?

They conduct a bunch of peace conferences pretending to make a difference.

Imagine that - a bunch of warmongers from around the world gather in a hall bearing their glaring badge of nationalistic separatism, and they talk about how to bring peace. What a joke!

You think conducting a bunch of phony peace conferences, completely disconnected from the soil, will solve everything! It won't!

You know why?

Because make-believe peacemaking is not the same as back-breaking peacemaking. To treat the pangs of this planet each civilian must stand up as peacemaker in their everyday life - each civilian must stand up as reformer - and not just any reformer. To reform this pest-infested planet only reformer won't do, what's needed is rowdy reformer. Rowdy Reformers by the hundreds, Rowdy Reformers by the thousands, that's what this world needs - not some backboneless, book-babbling intellectuals playing pretend peace with pretend intellect.

Be a Reformer,
Be a Rowdy!
And every inhuman that comes in your way,
Unarmed you set fire to their dormant
humanity.

3. Squatters of Earth

Until each bullet of imperialism, nationalism and fundamentalism is confronted by a volcanic heart of the civilian everywhere, there is no peace, there will never be peace.

World peace needs world citizens – it needs civilians who are, first, citizens of the world, then if the heart desires, citizens of their respective nations.

You see, I don't care for nationality, but you may. And that's perfectly fine. The point is, nationality is not the problem, nationalism is. In the same way, religion is not the problem, religious fundamentalism is.

You know why?

Because wherever an ideology claims supremacy, there it breeds terrorism. And such terrorism cannot be eliminated with armed intervention even in a million years.

Soldiers can eliminate terrorists, but only civilians can end terrorism - civilians who are responsible - civilians who are human first, and citizens of their nation second, if not never.

And as for the politicians - you think they are your representative right!

Let me tell you something.

They ain't!

They are just worthless squatters (no criticism to the exceptions) in an apartment which is driven and defended by civil servants and soldiers all along. Hence, the politicians are psychologically and professionally bound to count on your primitive sense of nationalism in order to survive.

But here's the thing.

As I said in my last work, you have to decide, do you want to live as ever-bickering concubines of pestilential politicians, or as an undivided planet's undivided civilians?

4.   The Political Dilemma

Nationalism is fodder for the politicians. Wipe out nationalism from your life, and you take away the very sustenance of the politicians. Thus you take away the very purpose behind their existence.

However, I am well aware that there are exceptions, that is, good politicians. But the point is, no politician can bring lasting reform in society until they renounce partisanism altogether.

For example, just today I heard another politician yell out loud to the members of her party, upon being appointed the Prime Minister, that her "party is the greatest political party on earth".

Now, as a behaviorist I haven't studied her behavior particularly, so I cannot comment whether she'll be a good leader to a people. She may, I don't know.

But the point is, until genuinely benevolent politicians work towards a nonpartisan society, no reform will last for long - the wheel of reform and deform will simply keep turning till kingdom come.

The day a politician acts nonpartisan, is the day politics disappears from earth - which, considering the behavioral tendencies of both the left and right wing politicians, I don't see happening any time soon.

I admit that the left has the moral and rational high ground, but unless the left forgets that they are left, every single reform they bring, will be overturned by the next right wing nincompoop that comes to power.

Hence, I lay my hopes and dreams in the hands of the civilians, not politicians - but not those pompous, arrogant, know-it-all and shallow civilians either.

I lay my hopes and dreams in the hands of those everyday, ordinary people who know in their very core, what does it mean to struggle for life – what does it mean to struggle for equality – what does it mean to struggle for an ounce of dignity, decency and amity.

5.   Representation is Regress

My dreams are entrusted to those civilians who don't walk away in the face of injustice - those who don't judge before ever trying to understand another - those who know that they know nothing, hence always keep learning - those who'd rather die than compromise their humanity.

Civilians, civilians, civilians - civilians alone will make the world, not politicians, not lawkeepers, not bureaucrats - just plain, ordinary civilians. And that, my friend, is the ultimate democracy we oughta aim for.

And such a democracy won't come from books - my books or anybody else' - they won't come from constitutions, and definitely not from scriptures.

A "smirt" guy once said, if you don't read books you have no advantage over those who can't read. Well, I can't even spell "smirt", and I say, read all you like - if you don't have the basic capacity to listen, you have no advantage over the animal.

Reading means nothing, if there is no realizing, if there is no feeling. If there is no genuine accountability on the part of the everyday, ordinary civilian, no policy, no constitution, no intellect, can instill and sustain reform and democracy in society.

Contrary to popular belief, democracy doesn't mean representative society, it means people driven society. The representation bit is only to be used as training wheel during the early decades of a democracy.

Let me put it another way. Representative democracy is a temporary part in the evolution of the human society, but it is not the ultimate paradigm of a human society.

Yet, indifferent and lazy citizens of a prehistorically divided planet have made representation the nucleus of democracy. Then like angry babies we yell, why do the politicians never rise above politics, making people their priority!

Thus, representative democracy of today is not a sign of progress, it is just a different kind of complacency. Hence, representation is but silent regress.

So the question is, how do we fix this?

Reform the politicians, you ensure reform in society for a few decades. Reform the citizens, you ensure reform in society for centuries.

And how do you reform the citizens - that is, how do we reform ourselves?

First and foremost, we gotta have a healthy hold over our animality - our primeval tendencies. We can't eliminate them mark you, for we can't eliminate basic biological drives that have been embedded in our neurophysiology through millions of years of evolution, but what we can do is be aware of them.

And with awareness comes the capacity for regulation - self-regulation that is. And a self-regulated civilian is the beginning of a self-regulated society.

6. Right Use of Arrogance

Primeval tendencies hold great potential, if you can learn to own them, regulate them and use them in your favor, rather than being owned, regulated and abused by them. Take arrogance for example.

Arrogance can be a great defense for dignity, but more often than less, we get wrapped up in its primeval tentacles through acts of narcissism.

Arrogance has its purpose, but first you gotta learn how to use it, so that it's a force for good, rather than a primeval tendency of self-aggrandizing.

Let me tell you a story. I was traveling to deliver a talk. The driver friend picked me up at the airport and dropped me at a fancy hotel booked by the organizers. At the reception before me there was an elderly couple. From what I gathered, their daughter had booked a room for them, but they were having a little difficulty communicating it.

I could sense that the hotel people at the desk didn't take them seriously to begin with, probably because they weren't dressed fancy. I kept quiet.

Finally the elderly man and woman gave up. They lowered their heads in disappointment and turned around to walk out without checking in. And just as their backs were turned, I heard one of the receptionists make the remark, "village idiots!"

That's it - I lost my cool! In that situation, at that moment, I felt as if my own parents were being treated like that.

I held the elderly gentleman by the wrist, marched up to the desk, and spoke.

"You think you are so fancy, don't you - working at a fancy place in your fancy clothes and phony etiquette - so much so that you forgot to treat people like people!

You ridicule them because they don't speak English.

Well, in that case, I speak more languages than you can count - then how should I treat you - you pathetic little tribal jerks!

It's not enough to wear clean clothes, go home and wash your heart with some soap. Despite all that cologne, you stink!

You can manage a hotel, you can manage a business, but you don't manage people, you treat them like family."

I would've went on and on, but the elderly person stopped me. Don't know whether the people at the reception realized their mistake, but by the look on their face they sure did feel small.

A moment later with a tinge of remorse and utter humility in voice, the other receptionist spoke. She apologized to the couple in their native tongue and finally helped them check in, without any miscommunication or frustration.

7. Where to Keep Your Lid On

Later when I went up to my room, the incident kept rewinding in my head due to my OCD. I needed closure, so I finished my rant at the receptionist in my head.

"What do you take me for!

Brain scientist here!

You know what it means?

It means I know your deepest fantasies as well as your darkest secrets - it means I know more about you than you know about yourself.

Yet have I ever belittled you?

Never!

You know why?

Because, by knowing the worst in you I came to now the best in you. Know your worst my friend - for once you conquer your worst you'll automatically manifest your best."

Finally, the compulsion faded, I felt calm, and went for a shower.

Anyway, the point is, an animal that claims to be human is still animal, whereas an animal that has conquered their animality is the first human.

Now let me tell you about another incident, where a similar humanitarian outburst was not necessary, for the circumstances did not involve active violation of rights of another, or even of myself for that matter, any more than the common criticism that I receive on a daily basis.

A pompous, arrogant, narcissistic intellectual came up to me at a conference and said rather boastfully.

"You must feel really good about yourself to be the nice guy all the time! But let me tell you something - it takes balls to say what's really on your mind. You might have heard, the best defense is a good offense..."

He went on and on for a while, and the more he spoke the more his intolerant nature became evident. I listened to everything he had to say, then heaved a soft sight, and replied with a smile.

"You are absolutely right! Ama senin gibi şerefsiz olmak insanın lazım yok - porque, no soy un hijo de puta como tú - nu okka chetta na kodakkala behave cheskovachhu, kaani naaku anthaa scene ledu."

He looked rather annoyed, because all my words went over his head, so he flared out, "don't beat around the bush, man - say, what you want to say!"

I spoke calmly. "I'd love to speak my mind, but I wouldn't want to give anyone an inferiority complex. Bad behavior don't make us cool, it only exposes the fool we are. If bad behavior made the world better, we'd already be living in utopia, instead of still struggling for basic human rights."

I didn't want the argument to linger any longer, so I asked him to join me for lunch. You see, self-regulation is not a sign of weakness, it's a sign of strength. It doesn't take any character for the animal to be animal, but the true test of character is to behave human, upon conquering our inner animal.

8.   World Leader, My Eye!

We are all born animals. The sooner we realize this, the sooner we can begin to be human. Self-aggrandizement doesn't make one human, self-regulation does - better yet, self-annihilation does.

Designation makes no leader, self-annihilation does - annihilation for the welfare of others, for the uplift of others.

Let's take the so-called leaders of the world for example.

World leader, my eye!

Hypocrites, every single one of them!

They attend climate conference emitting more carbon than all their citizens combined. They attend peace conference with nuclear codes handy in a briefcase.

And you want these two-timing morons to bring peace, health and harmony in the world! Keep dreaming - keep deluding yourself! I for one choose not to delegate the responsibility of my world to a bunch of windbags. The world is mine, its problems are mine.

Most of those in power would be offended by this statement of mine, save the rare few who genuinely care about social reform, and are well aware of the unscrupulous aspect of political life.

You see, until you are an actual revolutionary and a radical politician, it is only natural that you'd give in to certain traditional habits of political life, once you rise to power.

Let me give you an example.

I have been a firm supporter of Bernie for some time. But do you think, if he ever became President he would deny flying in the exclusive Air Force One, or deny himself the access to nuclear codes?

No need to answer, just think. This holds true for the nicest and brightest of politicians, like AOC, Ilhan and many more. But mark you, nobody would be happier than me, if I am proven wrong on this particular point.

I beg of you, my brave reformer – prove me wrong!

Anyway, this is why, I'd make a lousy politician, because politics demands compromise of principles, and I'd rather give up my life than give up my principles.

It is extremely easy to talk against power, when you don't have any. Once you achieve that power, that's when the real test of character begins.

This is not because people are innately evil and all that nonsense. This is just because the mind has an evolutionary predisposition to be swayed by luxury, power and comfort, without even being aware of it.

However, this is where a reformer differs from a run-of-the-mill politician.

9.   The Impossible Peacemaker

Counterfeit revolutionaries give in to the comfort and security of authoritarian life, the moment they come to power themselves. Upon coming to power, the most outspoken activist no longer minds getting acquainted with the nuclear codes of inhumanity, in the name of national security.

If asked why, their usual answer is - it's a necessary evil. Thus, an activist is only activist till they come to power. Once in power, most of them turn into the same kind of rotten politicians, that they have been fighting against.

That's human behavior 101 in relation to political revolution.

It is easy to fight power, when you have none, when you feel like the victim. The real battle begins when you start to have a taste of power.

It takes an impossible character to stand by their principles till their last breath, rejecting the pressure of oppression, as well as the convenience of power. For most it's much more convenient to just give in to the conveniences.

Therefore I say, I'll call a President Peacemaker, the day they sign the first executive order for nuclear disarmament. And I'll call the politicians peacemaker, when they work to turn that executive order into statutory law.

Because, let's face it - no politician in power has the guts to rock the status quo of nationalism-induced international squabbles - oops, I mean international relations!

So, if ever a nutcase reformer ends up the commander-in-chief of a nation, their first duty is to sign that executive order of peace. Because, peace isn't the work of politicians, peace is the work of reformers.

When politicians speaks, it's noise, when the reformer speaks, it's the rule - divine rule! Remember that. It is of great importance that you remember that. Because if the reformer loses heart, nobody can rescue the society from the ominous clutches of inhumanity.

This reformer could be a president, a representative, or they could be a plain, ordinary, everyday citizen. However, more often than less, you'll find a reformer amongst the commoners than the politicians.

The point is, in front of the radioactivity of a reformer heart, radioactivity of a hundred nuclear warheads turns dim. So, be that reformer, my friend – be that reformer.

If not you – who else!

Be that impossible peacemaker that this world desperately needs.

10. Playing Pretend Peace

When the heart turns radioactive with compassion, all war and warheads will become history. So why do we have so many nukes threatening the peace of this planet?

Simple - it's because the everyday, ordinary civilian heart is not radioactive yet - it's because the everyday, ordinary civilian heart is not radioactive with compassion yet - with conscience yet - with accountability yet.

That's why we like to play pretend development with the archaic nonsense of representation. Then those representatives attend peace conferences with nuclear codes in their pocket.

What a joke!

I'll say it plainly. Those who got no balls need the nuclear football. Nuclear reactor aquí! If it goes off, there is no remuneration, only annihilation - annihilation del degradation, annihilation del discrimination, annihilation del dehumanization.

Who am I?

Yo soy corazón calamidad.

Every heart that turns into a brakeless bulldozer in the face of inhumanity, is corazón calamidad. Every heart that turns into an unpluggable volcano in the face of bigoted barbarism, is corazón calamidad. Every heart that calls every other heart their family, and stands prepared to fight the almighty god if necessary, is corazón calamidad.

So I ask you - who are you?

This has nothing to do with law, this has nothing to do with policy, this has nothing to do with politicians, bureaucrats and law enforcement officers.

You know what it is all about?

It is about common, everyday, ordinary rightness - rightness that comes from the heart, not from the books, old or new - rightness that comes from realization, not indoctrination - rightness that comes from questioning, not memorizing.

11. Human Rightness

I am not here to tell you what is legally right, I can only tell you what is humanly right. All law must align themselves with human rightness, if they are to serve humanity at all, breaking free from their age-old inclinations of corruption.

I am not here to tell you what is spiritually right or religiously right, I can only tell you what is humanly right. All religion and spirituality must align themselves with human rightness, if they are to break free from their age-old habit of indoctrination and superstition.

And thus rises the fundamental principle of nation building - which is - there can be no modern nation, unless it severs all allegiance to institution - religious, legal, spiritual, political or any other.

Let me put it into perspective.

There is no such thing as a modern christian nation, modern islamic nation, modern hindu nation, modern atheist nation and so on. A modern nation is a secular nation, if not, it's not modern, but medieval.

Once you've realized this, the next realization is bound to come on its own – that is - there is no such thing as a modern planet with hundreds of nations. A modern planet is one nation, if not, it's not modern, but medieval.

And the only way to achieve this unification is to abandon all forms of allegiance from our mind, be it allegiance to logic, faith or anything else. And the interesting part here is, it is quite easy to observe the harms of religious allegiance, but not so easy to notice the harms of logic and reason.

So, I'll say it plainly, anybody who deems logic superior to life, is as dangerous as those who deem religion superior to life.

So how do we put life back in life?

How do we put life into society?

The answer is simple - with revolution.

12. Revolution By Heart

What's needed is revolution - unarmed, unbent, unyielding, unsophisticated, undoctrinated, and unreckless revolution. Mind you, those in power will always declare revolution as a threat to law and order, even if they came to power through revolution themselves.

Why?

Because revolution is a threat to corruption –and more importantly, revolution is a threat to authoritarianism.

So I say again, what's needed is revolution - not just any old reckless, mindless and heartless revolution like the January 6 insurrection - but revolution with heart, revolution with mind, revolution with conscience, courage and compassion, and most of all, revolution without arms.

Let me put this into perspective. Fever is not actually a sign of sickness, it is a sign that your body is fighting infection. Likewise, revolution is not a sign of disorder, it is a sign that the society is fighting the infection of inhumanity.

Fight the infection, my friend - fight the infection of inhumanity - because the moment you stop fighting the infection - then and there the world stops moving forward - then and there the world begins its descent - from the course of civilization to uncivilization - from the course of assimilation to asphyxiation.

13. Deadlier Than Terrorist

It's not enough to be yet another attention-seeking activist. You gotta be deadlier than the terrorist, and kindlier than Teresa. Only then the pestilential politicians will think twice before even dreaming of exploiting the people.

You see, everybody is a terrorist, till you see the reformist. Bring that reformer out my friend, in its full glory and ferociousness. Once you do, every time a politician or fundamentalist even dreams of doing something inhuman, a voice of caution will strike them from inside - don't you dare, kid - or else, they'll bring hell down on you - then you'll have neither the seat, nor the ass to sit on it!

Whatever you do, do it not just for yourself, but for all. Even an animal can live for itself, it takes a human to live for others. It takes a human to live for their kind - for humankind.

Let me put it to you another way. Anybody can be a coder, you for one, be a humanitarian coder. Anybody can be a scientist, you for one, be a humanitarian scientist. Anybody can be a scholar, you for one, be a humanitarian scholar. Anybody can be an entrepreneur, you for one, be a humanitarian entrepreneur.

I built my first circuit board, when I was eleven, without all the fancy resources available to the children in the west. But anybody can build a circuit, that's no biggie. Build a circuit that empowers a society - that my friend, is called humanitarian technology. And that's the kind of technology this world desperately needs.

The world needs the kind of technology that lifts human condition, yet what we mostly have today is technology that elevates human comfort and degrades human condition.

It won't do!

Open your eyes - look around - look at what reckless technology, driven by arrogant intelligence, has done to the world!

And you know why?

Because, with superior sentience, come superior screw-ups. And this holds particularly true for industrialization.

14. Reject Less, Repair More

Even if we put aside carbon emission, in the year 2020 alone humankind has produced over 2 billion tonnes of trash, which is expected to rise over 70% by the year 2050.

Thus, in the name of progress we the gadget-mad gargoyles keep acting as the true eco-terrorists of the glorious dumping ground, called the planet earth. 2% of all our waste is e-waste. And the alarming bit here is that, that 2% e-waste comprises over 70% of our overall toxic waste.

So, what can you do, you ask? Simple - reject less, repair more. Try to make things last as long as possible, or pass them on to those who have need for them. Don't let things go to waste, just because you can afford new ones.

For example, my kid cousin's laptop has been acting up for some time now. But instead of buying them a new pc, I ordered the replacement for the faulty part and repaired the laptop myself. This way, we not only reduce our e-waste footprint on the planet, but in the process, we teach kids to value things.

The point is, whether you do it yourself or get it done by a professional, by practicing repair, you are actively participating in the making of a greener, cleaner and healthier world.

It's not enough to be just a consumer, you gotta be a conscious consumer, otherwise there is no difference between a consumer and a slave. That is why, right-to-repair is not only a human rights issue, it is also an environmental issue. Repairing and recycling are the bedrock of sustainability. So I say again - reject less, repair more.

Amazingly enough, this holds true not just for possessions, but also for people. In a way, we've become so obsessed with possessions that we give up more easily on people than possessions.

As I once said, we are supposed to love people, and use possessions, yet in sheer stupidity, we continue to love possessions and use people.

This has to change. This must change. It is not merely a matter of moral choice, rather it is a matter of existential necessity.

People, people, people - this should be on our mind 24/7.

Society, society, society - this oughta be on our mind 24/7.

And in doing so, if we are confronted even with death a thousand times, let us do so without flinching an eyelid.

15. Bullets Don't Kill The Being

Bullets only kill the body, not the being. The being lives, so long as the cause lives - so long as the idea lives.

But here, I must mention something rather quintessential. You see, this particular statement, does not apply to you if you have a family to support.

I told you a thousand times, if I told you once - you gotta be flexible around ideas. You gotta embrace them in your life, the way it suits you the best, without submitting to self-centricity that is.

As a behaviorist let me tell you a secret.

I can make such radical statements because I am single, and more importantly, I don't have children of my own. And I do ardently wish that I kick the bucket before I even get to start a family of my own, even though a part of me still wants to start a family someday.

Because once I do have children of my own, if I ever do that is, my radical nature is bound to mellow, to some extent at least. I say, mellow, mark you, not compromised.

So the point is this.

If you have a family to support, you gotta play it smart while standing up to inhumanity - not safe, but smart. Idealism has no place in real life. You mustn't take anybody's words too literally, not even mine. Look at what literalism has done to the fundamentalists. I don't want you to make the same mistake as them. And more importantly, I don't want to be the cause of the horrors brought along by such mistake.

This is where reason becomes relevant. You must always reason, how exactly certain ideas apply to your life, and then adopt them accordingly.

This is not compromise, this is called the rightful realization of ideas - the rightful manifestation and application of ideas.

Stand up to inhumanity, but do so mindfully.

Let me put to you another way.

Turning away is not an option, but how you stand up to inhumanity, that is completely up to you. Main thing is to not stay silent - main thing is to not stay complacent - main thing is to not stay indifferent.

16. Once The Civilians Grow Up

Justice begins when civilians rise. And when civilians rise, governments fall. As I said in my last work, government is a dream, and civilians are the dreamer. The dream exists so long as the dreamer is asleep.

There is no such thing good government and bad government. The fact that government exists is the sign of a backboneless citizenry. Once the citizens actually act like citizens, and take the responsibility of their society on their shoulders, rather than delegating it to the so-called elected representatives, there will be no trace of government whatsoever.

But then again, I am no idealist. I am a behaviorist, which means that I am dutybound to acknowledge the realities of human nature as well as the possibilities.

So I am compelled to say - right now the absence of government would only bring chaos.

On top of that, no state would willingly work towards its own abolition.

So, if the government ever disappears at all, it won't happen by means of policy, or military coup, it can happen only by civilian intervention - by everyday, ordinary civilian intervention.

When the civilians have grown out of the need for government, and are capable enough to carry the responsibility of their society on their own, there will be no reason for the state to exist. Thus, having served their brief role in the evolution of society, all constructs of state, government and representation will go extinct on their own - just like the tail on our back disappeared when we had no use for them, once we started to walk upright on our feet, breaking free from our traditional habit of hanging from the trees.

17. Policy Makes No Planet

Democracy shall never truly evolve by means of policy. I am not saying, policy isn't relevant. Of course it is, at our current evolutionary stage that is.

But what I am pointing out is far simpler than that.

What I am saying is this.

Society is reformed by the intervention of the civilians, not by the initiative of the state.

In short, every civilian, every so-called commoner must become a reformer of their part of the world, only then society will be humanized. Better die a roaring reformer than live as a cowardly conformer.

Let me put this into perspective.

A scholar friend of mine said to me the other day, 'would you please wipe that ridiculously naive smile off your face - and, isn't it time, you start dressing like a proper thinker!'

With a grin on my lips I replied.

'People dress fancy because either consciously or subconsciously they feel the urge to impress others.

Upon sacrificing my youth, my life, my every last trace of sleep, sanity and serenity, in the service of humanity, I have neither the urge to impress nor the desire to prove anybody anything. All are my children*, and it's the children who feel the urge to impress their parents, not the other way around.'

(*With the possible exception of one, which I might have to make someday - I don't know who, but to her I shall be a slave.)

And this, my friend, is how the civilians are to treat the so-called administrators of a society. It's the civilians who are the real administrators of a nation, those in government, are mere underlings, whether they are elected representatives or graduated bureaucrats.

18. The Way is Civilian

Law and policy are an aid to civic duty, not a substitute. So I repeat – deadlier than terrorist, kindlier than Teresa - that's how we'll reform the world. Every civilian must become more dangerous than the terrorist, more compassionate than Teresa, and more conscientious than Tesla.

Only then the politicians and bureaucrats will think twice before harassing and exploiting the civilians. All partisanism will wither in front of the resolve of such civilians. In the face of such reformer civilians, even the politicians themselves will forget which party they belong to, so will their next of kin.

Remember, my would-be patriots of the planet - revolutionary is the revolution, pedestrian is the path, and the civilized is civilization.

Everything good starts with you, and everything bad must end with you.

Like it or not, every single one of us has descended either from the oppressors of planet earth, or from the oppressed of planet earth. Now the question is, do you have the capacity to start afresh, renouncing the desire for conquest, as well as the desire for vengeance!

If you do, only then shall there be peace - only then shall there be civilization - only then shall it be a society of civilized amiables, rather than suited animals.

19. Why I am Human
(The Sonnet)

Why I am Human
(The Sonnet)

Some explain why they are catholic,
Some explain why they are atheist,
Some explain why they are muslim,
Some explain why they are socialist.

Some explain why they are jew,
Some explain why they are buddhist,
Some explain why they are hindu,
Some explain why they are humanist.

I heard plenty people explain,
Why they are what they are,
But I'm yet to hear one person say,
First I am human, all else later.

What is this mad obsession with all the ism!
Why can't we be just human, plain and simple!

20. Virtue No Ism
(The Sonnet)

Virtue No Ism
(The Sonnet)

What is this obsession with ism before human!
Why are we still catering to ancestral stupidity!
Are we really gonna let their shortsightedness,
To define our capacity, character and destiny!
Some of them might have had the vision of unity,
Hence they spoke of peace and neighborly love.
But most lacked the sight to live beyond ism,
And we continue to prioritize ism over love.
No ideology has a monopoly over virtue,
Virtues are born of mind, not ideology.
Yet all ideologies try to codify virtue,
By doing so they only vilify all virtuosity.
All virtues are but the descendants of love.
To codify virtue is to ruin the universality of love.

21. Representation is Degradation
(The Sonnet)

Representation is Degradation
(The Sonnet)

Nationalism is but a precursor to fascism,
Representation is but a precursor to corruption.
Delegation is but a precursor to destitution,
Law-abidance is but a precursor to degradation.
Representation without accountability is just,
As undemocratic as taxation without representation.
Trading in one party for another is not change,
But merely the re-initiation of prehistoric division.
Democracy that shows no sign of nonpartisanism,
Is but a petri dish of prejudice most blinding.
Such a democracy stuck on representation,
Is but a silent dictatorship in the making.
Neither law nor party loyalty will elevate the society.
All my hope, therefore, lies upon civilian responsibility.

22. Time To Bury All Divide
(The Sonnet)

Time to Bury All Divide
(The Sonnet)

It's time we bury the nationality nonsense,
Person is known by their behavior not nation.
It's time we bury the holy book nonsense,
Person becomes holy by compassion not religion.
It's time we bury the representation nonsense,
Social reform starts with civic duty not delegation.
It's time we bury the intellectualism nonsense,
Society is civilized by heart not cocky argumentation.
It's time we abolish the royalty nonsense,
Humans are known by behavior, animals by bloodline.
It's time we dissolve all moronity of hierarchy,
True advancement lies in the abolition of divide.
Even the mighty sun doesn't differentiate
between first world and third world humanity.
It is only the lowly beings who can't help
but practice some good old exclusivity.

23. I Don't Know (The Sonnet)

I Don't Know

(The Sonnet)

What does winning or losing mean,
I don't know.
What does kill or be killed mean,
I don't know.
What does 'my culture, your culture' mean,
I don't know.
What does 'my nation, your nation' mean,
I don't know.
What does 'my people, your people' mean,
I don't know.
What does my life and your life mean,
I don't know.
I only know, we are not some mindless mouthpiece
for our dead ancestors and their shortsightedness.
It is time we bury the divisionism that
they passed on to us tradition and heritage.

24. Gods by The Hundreds
(The Sonnet)

Gods by The Hundreds
(The Sonnet)

Some people fear christ,
Some claim to hear christ.
I work restless day and night,
To raise the living christs.
Some people fear god,
Some claim to be prophets.
I work without sleep and rest,
To raise gods by the hundreds.
One week of my life produces enough electricity,
To power a 100 years of humanitarian endeavor.
One life laid down to lift up the society,
Triggers a wildfire of sacrificial fervor.
I am but an instrument in the making of legends.
I am but a matchstick to light up the sapiens.

25. Sonnet of Superpowers

Sonnet of Superpowers

Poet's superpower is their pain,
Philosopher's superpower is reason.
Scientist's superpower is their brain,
Artist's superpower is their vision.
Janitor's superpower is cleanliness,
Hooker's superpower is practical piety.
Bartender's superpower is resilience,
Teacher's superpower is curiosity.
Entrepreneur's superpower is stubbornness,
Engineer's superpower is "unsliding caliber".
Copper's superpower oughta be unbent backbone,
Astronaut's superpower is conquest of fear.
Humankind's superpower is diversity.
Life's superpower is plasticity.

26. Reformer Needed
(The Sonnet)

Reformer Needed
(The Sonnet)

To put the politicians straight,
What's needed is a reformer.
To put the soldiers straight,
What's needed is a reformer.
To put the scientists straight,
What's needed is a reformer.
To put the philosophers straight,
What's needed is a reformer.
To put the entrepreneurs straight,
What's needed is a reformer.
To put the preachers straight,
What's needed is a reformer.
And how does the reformer remain straight,
By looking beyond the beliefs of binary lanes.

27. Martyr for Humanity
(The Sonnet)

Martyr for Humanity
(The Sonnet)

I am not a writer, I am an anomaly,
For writers run empty after a few works.
I lost count of mine a long time ago,
Yet I keep imploding with no sign of cork.
My brain keeps making appointments,
That my body can't keep without crashing.
I am not finished with one work,
And lo, another one starts pouring!
Someone, please calm my brain!
The torture grows excruciating by the minute!
Any day now hopefully an artery will blow,
Then I shall finally have my eternal rest.
Once I am gone, don't go making a cult out of me.
I shall be alive, so long as there is one human
standing ready to be martyred for humanity.

28. Soil, The Sonnet

Soil, The Sonnet

My skin is the color of soil,
My covers are the color of soil.
My heart is the color of soil,
My blood is the color of soil.

Species that forgets the soil,
Is a lifeform abandoned by nature.
Species that values sales over soil,
Will soon be vaporized or drowned by nature.

If we have no place for soil in our heart,
How can we expect the soil to replenish us!
If we have no place for nature in our heart,
How can we expect nature to have a place for us!

Only soil is real, all else is delusion.
Advancement that has no regard for the soil,
is but aneurysm destined for degeneration.

29. What is Sapiens
(The Sonnet)

What is Sapiens
(The Sonnet)

Soil can survive without sapiens,
But there is no sapiens without soil.
There is no us if nature goes off the rocker,
Yet way more than nature, we value gas and oil.
We started off using clothes as cover for privacy,
And we ended up prioritizing clothes over integrity.
Instead of loving people and using the products,
We ended up loving products and abusing humanity.
Sapiens is supposed to mean wise and aware,
But in practice, sapiens is code for shallow.
Sapiens has become just a synonym for show-off.
Neither wise, nor aware, sapiens just means narrow.
However, no error is ultimate if we're willing for reform.
An expanding heart is the antidote to all narrow norm.

30. Curves, Clothes, Character
(The Sonnet)

Curves, Clothes, Character
(The Sonnet)

Your abs won't last, your racks won't last,
Eventually everything ends up in wrinkle.
Polish the outside all you want but,
All curves are crookery if the heart is wrinkled.
Slimness is not the same as fitness,
Skinship is not the same as kinship.
Etiquettes don't elevate the world,
Apparels don't bring liberty and leadership.
Waste not the life on measuring your waist,
All waist is waste if the backbone is malnourished.
Fitness is fiction when shallowness runs rampant,
All curves are filth if the being remains prejudiced.
Curves and clothes have no bearing on character whatsoever.
Better a character out of shape, than a shape without character.

31. Tenet Beyond Tongue
(The Sonnet)

Tenet Beyond Tongue
(The Sonnet)

Kalbin olduğu her yerde kader var,
Aşkın olduğu her yerde umut var.
Mücadelenin olduğu her yerde mucize var,
İnsanlığın olduğu her yerde ilahiyat var.

Donde hay corazón, hay destino,
Esperanza es el niño del amor.
Donde hay lucha por la vida hay milagro,
Divinidad es el reflejo del humano.

No matter how many tongues we say it in,
The fact still remains all the same.
Where there is heart there is everything,
Without heart divinity, intellect all are lame.

Biz kimiz? İnsanız. ¿Quienes somos? Humanos.
Who are we? Humanity. Our purpose?
Ayudar a los humanos.

32. Blasphemy (The Sonnet)

Blasphemy
(The Sonnet)

Insan dertte olduğunda,
Sen ve ben yok, sadece biz varız.
Birbirimize destek olamıyorsa,
Biz insan değiliz, sadece hayvanız.

İnsan merhameti unuttuğunda,
Cennet, cehennem, hepsi aynı.
İnsan insanın acılarına ilaç olamıyorsa,
İnsan, hayvan, hepsi aynı.

When another being is in pain,
Only blasphemy is indifference.
If we can't be cure to each other,
It's not life, but derangement.

In wiping out the world's tears,
I lost touch with the excitement of youth.
In bringing smiles on forgotten faces,
I discovered myself anew.

Dünyanın gözyaşlarını silmek için
gençliğimi bile feda ettim.
Çünkü insanların gülüşünde
ben kendimi kaybettim.

33. Young, Boiling, Selfless
(The Sonnet)

Young, Boiling, Selfless
(The Sonnet)

Sen söyle karadeniz,
Ben daha ne yapayım!
Gençliğimi feda ettim,
Hayatımı feda ettim,
Ben daha ne yapayım!
In wiping out the anguish of society,
I forgot to indulge in the exploits of youth.
Once I realized the world on my shoulder,
That was the end of self, and the birth of truth.
People dream of earning a ton of money,
I always dreamed of earning immortality.
Anybody can live in flesh and blood,
Mark of character is to live in people's memory.
An eye for an eye makes the whole world blind,
But a life given for a life fallen
makes the whole world alive.

34. No Teacher for Present
(The Sonnet)

No Teacher for Present
(The Sonnet)

Life's purpose is realization of life,
Beyond the narrowness of yesterday.
Instead of waiting for a fictitious future,
Life is whatever you make of it today.
The past is always afraid of the future,
Don't let their fear ruin your present.
The future may be condescending to the past,
Don't let such arrogance ruin your humanness.
Embrace the wonders that the past has to offer,
Learn from their blunders even through their denial.
Be mindful of the direction that you are headed,
Then leap to work on the present, lock, stock 'n barrel.
Neither past nor future is qualified to teach the present.
All present must find their way free from all allegiance.

35. Love who you like
(The Sonnet)

Love who you like
(The Sonnet)

Love who you like,
Wear what you like.
Have kids when you like,
Above all, live as you like.
Only thing that matters is that,
You don't fan the flames of hurt.
The only gospel of life is that,
There is no other gospel but love.
Obscene mind finds obscenity everywhere,
For the outside is but a reflection of the inside.
Less of the pomposity and more of the character,
That is how we shall harness our forces civilized.
I only know of one holiness, it's called kindness.
Without it, all scriptures are scum,
and all courts are incognizant.

36. Women Know Best
(The Sonnet)

Women Know Best
(The Sonnet)

Wanna learn about running a world, go find a woman mentor,
For women are better teacher and better leader.
Society that glorifies men and objectifies women,
Is but a jungle where primitivity never ceases to fester.
Nature looks upon kindly any species that,
Has realized the synonymity of sacred and feminine.
Those who still fail to recognize the voice of women,
Are basically violating the very reason for existing.
Women know best what's best for the world,
The world that comes out of her womb.
They cuss us, they mock us, it's for our own good,
All time is feminine, feminine is the rule.
The world is but creation, women are the creator.
Feminine is the idol, we are mere idolator.

37. The Sapiens Experiment
(A Sonnet)

The Sapiens Experiment
(A Sonnet)

If knowledge is power,
Love is superpower.
If curiosity is a gift,
Compassion is a trove of treasure.

More than abundance, focus on wholeness,
More than serenity, focus on simplicity.
More than leading, focus on service,
More than individuality, focus on collectivity.

To reason is great, but to accept is greater,
To be loved is great, but to be love is greater.
To have help is great, but to be the help is greater,
To seek light is great, but to be the light is greater.

Sapiens are the most spectacular experiment of nature,
To waste it all on presumptions is but sheer disaster.

BIBLIOGRAPHY

Archer M., (2000), Being Human: The Problem of Agency. Cambridge University Press.

Adolphs R (2003) Cognitive neuroscience of human social behaviour. Nature Rev Neurosci 4: 165–178.

Adolphs R, Tranel D, Damasio AR (2003) Dissociable neural systems for recognizing emotions. Brain Cogn 52: 61–69.

Andresen, Jensine, and Robert Forman, eds. Cognitive Models and Spiritual Maps. Bowling Green, Ohio: Imprint Academic, 2000.

Azari, Nina, Janpeter Nickel, Gilbert Wunderlich, Michael Niedeggen, Harald Hefter, Lutz Tellmann, Hans Herzog, Petra Stoerig, Dieter Birnbacher, and Rudiger Seitz. "Neural Correlates of Religious Experience."

European Journal of Neuroscience 13, no. 8 (2001)

Agar, N. (2004). Liberal eugenics: In defence of human enhancement. London: Blackwell Publishing.

Alteheld, N., Roessler, G., Vobig, M., & Walter, R. (2004). The retina implant new approach to a visual prosthesis. Biomedizinische Technik, 49(4), 99–103.

Antal, A., Nitsche, M. A., Kincses, T. Z., Kruse, W., Hoffmann, K. P., & Paulus, W. (2004a). Facilitation of visuo-motor learning by transcranial direct current stimulation of the motor and extrastriate visual areas in humans. European Journal of Neuroscience, 19(10), 2888–2892.

Bernstein R.J., (1971), Praxis and Action: Contemporary Philosophies of Human Activity. Philadelphia: University of Pennsylvania Press.

Bernstein R.J., (1976), The Restructuring Social and Political Thought.

Bernstein R.J., (1983), Beyond Relativism and Objectivism: Science, Hermeneutics, and Praxis. Philadelphia: University of Pennsylvania Press.

Bernstein R.J., (1986), Philosophical Profiles. Philadelphia: University of Pennsylvania Press.

Bernstein R.J., (1991), New Constellation. Cambridge: MIT Press.

Birkhead, T. R., Johnson, S. D. & Nettleship, D. N. (1985). Extra-pair matings and mate guarding in the common murre Uria aalge. - Anim. Behav. 33, p. 608-619.

Beauregard, Mario, and Vincent Paquette. "Neural Correlates of a Mystical Experience in Carmelite Nuns." Neuroscience Letters 405, no. 3 (2006)

Benson, Herbert. Timeless Healing: The Power and Biology of Belief. New York: Scribner, 1996

Bose, Subhas Chandra. An Indian Pilgrim: An Unfinished Autobiography, Oxford University Press, 1997

Bogen, J.E.(1995a), 'On the neurophysiology of consciousness: Part I. An overview', Consciousness and Cognition, 4.

Bogen, J.E. (1995b), 'On the neurophysiology of consciousness: Part II. Constraining the semantic problem', Consciousness and Cognition, 4.

Bremner, J. D., R. Soufer, et al. (2001). "Gender differences in cognitive and neural correlates of remembrance of emotional words." Psychopharmacol Bull 35 (3).

Brothers, L. (2002). The social brain: A project for integrating primate behavior and neurophysiology in a new domain. In J. T. Cacioppo et al. (Eds.), Foundations in neuroscience. Cambridge, MA: MIT Press.

Buss, D. D. (2003). Evolutionary Psychology: The New Science of Mind, 2nd ed. New York: Allyn & Bacon.

Buss, D. M. (1989). "Conflict between the sexes: Strategic interference and the evocation of anger and upset." J Pers Soc Psychol 56 (5).

Buss, D. M. (1995). "Psychological sex differences. Origins through sexual selection." Am Psychol 50 (3).

Buss, D. M., and D. P. Schmitt (1993). "Sexual strategies theory: An evolutionary perspective on human mating." Psychol Rev 100 (2).

Blakemore SJ, Decety J (2001) From the perception of action to the understanding of intention. Nature Rev Neurosci 2: 561.

Colapietro V., (1988), "Human Agency: The Habits of Our Being." Southern Journal of Philosophy, XXVI, 2, pp. 153-68.

Colapietro V., (1992), "Purpose, Power, and Agency." The Monist, 75, 4 (October) pp. 423-44.

Colapietro V., (2004a), "C. S. Peirce's Reclamation of Teleology." Nature in American Philosophy, ed. Jean De Groot (Washington, D.C.: Catholic University Press of America), pp. 88-108.

Carey DP, Perrett DI, Oram MW (1997) Recognizing, understanding and reproducing actions. In: Jeannerod M, Grafman J (eds) Handbook of neuropsychology. Vol. 11: Action and cognition. Elsevier, Amsterdam.

Carr L, Iacoboni M, Dubeau MC, Mazziotta JC, Lenzi GL (2003) Neural mechanisms of empathy in humans: a relay from neural systems for imitation to limbic areas. Proc Natl Acad Sci USA 100: 5497–5502.

Chomsky Noam, (2017) Requiem for the American Dream

Chomsky Noam, (2016) Who Rules the World?

Chomsky Noam, (2010) How the World Works

Churchland, P.S. (1986), Neurophilosophy (Cambridge, MA: The MIT Press).

Churchland, P.S. & Ramachandran, V.S. (1993), 'Filling in: Why Dennett is wrong', in Dennett and His Critics: Demystifying Mind, ed. B. Dahlbom (Oxford: Blackwell Scientific Press).

Churchland, P.S., Ramachandran, V.S. & Sejnowski, T.J. (1994), 'A critique of pure vision', in Large- scale Neuronal Theories of the Brain, ed. C. Koch & J.L. Davis (Cambridge, MA: The MIT Press).

Coyle EF. Integration of the physiological factors determining endurance performance ability. Exerc Sport Sci Rev. 1995;23:25–63.

Crick, F. (1994), The Astonishing Hypothesis: The Scientific Search for the Soul (New York: Simon and Schuster).

Crick, F. (1996), 'Visual perception: rivalry and consciousness', Nature, 379.

Crick, F. & Koch, C. (1992), 'The problem of consciousness', Scientific American, 267.

Damasio, A (2003a) Looking for Spinoza. Harcourt Inc. Damasio A (2003b) Feeling of emotion and the self. Ann NY Acad Sci 1001: 253–261.

d'Aquili, Eugene. "Senses of Reality in Science and Religion." Zygon 17, no 4 (1982)

d'Aquili, Eugene. "The Biopsychological Determinants of Religious Ritual Behavior." Zygon 10, no. 1 (1975)

d'Aquili, Eugene. "The Myth-Ritual Complex: A Biogenetic Structural Analysis." Zygon 18, no. 3 (1983)

d'Aquili, Eugene, and Andrew Newberg. The Mystical Mind: Probing the Biology of Religious Experience. Minneapolis: Fortress Press, 1999.

Daly DD. 1958. Ictal affect. Am J Psychiatry.

Damasio, A. (1994) Descartes' Error: Emotion, Reason and the Human Brain. New York, Putnams.

Damasio, A. (1999) The Feeling of What Happens: Body, Emotion and the Making of Consciousness. London, Heinemann.

Darwin, C. (1859) On the Origin of Species by Means of Natural Selection. London, Murray.

Darwin, C. (1871) The Descent of Man and Selection in Relation to Sex. London, John Murray.

Darwin, C. (1872) The Expression of the Emotions in Man and Animals. London, John Murray; also published 1965, Chicago, University of Chicago Press.

Dawkins, M.S. (1987) Minding and mattering. In C. Blakemore and S. Greenfield (eds) Mindwaves. Oxford, Blackwell, 151-60.

Dawkins, R. (1976) The Selfish Gene. Oxford, Oxford University Press; a new edition, with additional material, was published in 1989.

Di Pellegrino G, Fadiga L, Fogassi L, Gallese V, Rizzolatti G (1992) Understanding motor events: A neurophysiological study. Exp Brain Res 91: 176–80.

Deikman, A.J. (2000) A functional approach to mysticism. Journal of Consciousness Studies 7(11-12), 75-91.

Delmonte, M.M. (1987) Personality and meditation. In M. West (ed.) The Psychology of Meditation. Oxford, Clarendon Press, 118-32.

Dennett, D.C. (1988) Quining qualia. In A.J. Marcel and E. Bisiach (eds) Consciousness in Contemporary Science. Oxford, Oxford University Press, 42-77.

Dennett, D.C. (1991) Consciousness Explained. Boston, MA, and London, Little, Brown and Co.

Dennett, D.C. (1995a) Darwin's Dangerous Idea. London, Penguin.

Dennett, D.C. (1998b) Brainchildren: Essays on Designing Minds. Cambridge, MA, MIT Press.

Dewhurst, Kenneth, and A. W. Beard. "Sudden Religious Conversions in Temporal Lobe Epilepsy." British Journal of Psychiatry 117 (1970)

Dewhurst K, Beard AW. Sudden religious conversions in temporal lobe epilepsy. 1970 Epilepsy Behav 2003

Devinsky O, Lai G. Spirituality and religion in epilepsy. Epilepsy Behav 2008.

Devinsky, O., Morrell, MJ, Vogt, BA. (1995) 'Contribution of anterior cingulate cortex to behavior', Brain, 118.

E. Horvitz, "One Hundred Year Study on Artificial Intelligence: Reflections and Framing," ed: Stanford University, 2014.

Eckhart Meister, Selected Writings

Egidi R., ed. (1999), "Von Wright and 'Dante's Dream': Stages in a Philosophical Pilgrim's Progress", in

In Search of a New Humanism: the Philosophy of G.H. von Wright, ed. by R. Egidi, Kluwer, Dordrecht.

Fadiga L, Fogassi L, Pavesi G, Rizzolatti G (1995) Motor facilitation during action observation: a magnetic stimulation study. J Neurophysiol 73: 2608–2611.

Fogassi L, Gallese V, Fadiga L, Rizzolatti G (1998) Neurons responding to the sight of goal directed hand/arm actions in the parietal area PF (7b) of the macaque monkey. Soc Neurosci Abs 24:257.5.

Frith U, Frith CD (2003) Development and neurophysiology of mentalizing. Philos Trans R Soc Lond B Biol Sci 358: 459.

Farah, M.J. (1989), 'The neural basis of mental imagery', Trends in Neurosciences, 10.

Finlay BL, Darlington RB (1995) Linked regularities in the development and evolution of mammalian brains. Science 268.

Freud, S. "The Interpretation of Dreams", 1900

Freud, S. "Selected papers on hysteria and other psychoneuroses" Journal of Nervous and Mental Disease 1909.

Freud, S. "The Origin and Development of Psychoanalysis", 1910

Freud, S. "Psychopathology of everyday life", 1914

Freud, S. "Beyond the Pleasure Principle", 1920

Frith, C.D. & Dolan, R.J. (1997), 'Abnormal beliefs: Delusions and memory', Paper presented at the May, 1997, Harvard Conference on Memory and Belief.

Gay, Volney, ed. Neuroscience and Religion. Plymouth, UK: Lexington Books, 2009.

Gazzaniga, M. S. (1985). The social brain. New York: Basic Books.

Gazzaniga, M.S. (1993), 'Brain mechanisms and conscious experience', Ciba Foundation Symposium, 174.

Geschwind N. "Behavioural changes in temporal lobe epilepsy". Psychol Med. 1979.

Gellhorn, E., Kiely, W.F. "Mystical states of consciousness: neurophysiological and clinical aspects." J Nerv Ment Dis. 1972;154:399-405.

Gilbert SL, Dobyns WB, Lahn BT (2005) Genetic links between brain development and brain evolution. Nat Rev Genet 6.

Gray JA. The Psychology of Fear and Stress. 2nd ed. New York, NY: Cambridge University Press; 1988.

Gloor, P. (1992), 'Amygdala and temporal lobe epilepsy', in The Amygdala: Neurobiological Aspects of Emotion, Memory and Mental Dysfunction, ed J.P. Aggleton (New York: Wiley-Liss).

Greenspan, S. I. and S. G. Shanker (2004). The first idea: How symbols, language, and intelligence evolved from our early primate ancestors to modern humans. Cambridge, MA: Da Capo Press.

Grady, D. (1993), 'The vision thing: Mainly in the brain', Discover, June.

Gallagher HL, Frith CD (2003) Functional imaging of 'theory of mind'. Trends Cogn Sci 7: 77.

Gallese V, Fogassi L, Fadiga L, Rizzolatti G (2002) Action representation and the inferior parietal lobule. In: Prinz W, Hommel B (eds) Attention & Performance XIX. Common mechanisms in perception and action. Oxford University Press, Oxford.

Gallese V, Keysers C, Rizzolatti G (2004) A unifying view of the basis of social cognition. Trends Cogn Sci 8: 396–403.

Goldman AI, Sripada CS (2004) Simulationist models of face-based emotion recognition. Cognition 94: 193–213.

Grèzes J, Costes N, Decety J (1998) Top-down effect of strategy on the perception of human biological motion: a PET investigation. Cogn Neuropsychol 15: 553–582.

Grèzes J, Armony JL, Rowe J, Passingham RE (2003) Activations related to "mirror" and "canonical" neurones in the human brain: an fMRI study. Neuroimage 18: 928–937.

Gross CG, Rocha-Miranda CE, Bender DB (1972) Visual properties of neurons in the inferotemporal cortex of the macaque. J Neurophysiol 35: 96–111.

Guevara Che, The Motorcycle Diaries, 1992

Hari R, Forss N, Avikainen S, Kirveskari S, Salenius S, Rizzolatti G (1998) Activation of human primary motor cortex during action observation: a neuromagnetic study. Proc. Natl Acad Sci USA 95: 15061–15065.

Hardy, G. H. (1940). Ramanujan. Cambridge: Cambridge University Press.

Hall, Daniel, Keith Meador, and Harold Koenig. "Measuring Religiousness in Health Research: Review and Critique." Journal of Religion and Health 47, no. 2 (2008)

Harris, Sam, Jonas Kaplan, Ashley Curiel, Susan Bookheimer, Marco Iacoboni, and Mark Cohen. "The Neural Correlates of Religious and

Nonreligious Belief." PLoS One 4, no. 10 (October 1, 2009)

Halgren, E. (1992), 'Emotional neurophysiology of the amygdala within the context of human cognition', in The Amygdala: Neurobiological Aspects of Emotion, Memory and Mental Dysfunction, ed J.P. Aggleton (New York: Wiley-Liss).

Halligan PW, Fink GR, Marshal JC, Vallar G. 2003. Spatial cognition: evidence from visual neglect. Trends Cogn Sci.

Handbook of Emotions, Edited by Michael Lewis, Jeannette M. Haviland-Jones, and Lisa Feldman Barrett, The Guilford Press; 3rd edition (2010).

Hameroff, S.R. and Penrose, R. (1996) Conscious events as orchestrated space-time selections. Journal of Consciousness Studies 3(1), 36-53; also reprinted in J. Shear (ed.) (1997) Explaining Consciousness-The Hard

Problem. Cambridge, MA, MIT Press, 177-95.

Harding, D.E. (1961) On Having no Head: Zen and the Re-Discovery of the Obvious. London, Buddhist Society.

Hardy, A. (1979) The Spiritual Nature of Man: A Study of Contemporary Religious Experience. Oxford, Clarendon Press.

Harre, R. and Gillett, G. (1994) The Discursive Mind. Thousand Oaks, CA, Sage.

Haugeland, J. (ed.) (1997) Mind Design II: Philosophy, Psychology, Artificial Intelligence. Cambridge, MA, MIT Press.

Hauser, M.D. (2000) Wild Minds: What Animals Really Think. New York, Henry Holt and Co.; London, Penguin.

Hebb, D.O. (1949) The Organization of Behavior. New York, Wiley.

Helmholtz, H.L.F. von (1856-67) Treatise on Physiological Optics.

Hess, EH (1975) "The role of pupil size in communication," Scientific American, 233(5), 110–12.

Heyes, C.M. (1998) Theory of mind in nonhuman primates. Behavioral and Brain Sciences 21, 101-48; with commentaries.

Heyes, C.M. and Galef, B.G. (eds) (1996) Social Learning in Animals: The Roots of Culture. San Diego, CA, Academic Press.

Hilgard, E.R. (1986) Divided Consciousness: Multiple Controls in Human Thought and Action. New York, Wiley.

Hilton, E.N., Lundberg, T.R. Transgender Women in the Female Category of Sport: Perspectives on Testosterone Suppression and Performance Advantage. Sports Med 51, 199–214 (2021).

Hitler, Adolf. Mein Kampf, 1925

Hodgson, R. (1891) A case of double consciousness. Proceedings of the Society for Psychical Research 7, 221-58.

Hofstadter, D.R. and Dennett, D.C. (eds) (1981) The Mind's I: Fantasies and Reflections on Self and Soul. London, Penguin.

Holland, J. (ed.) (2001) Ecstasy: The Complete Guide: A Comprehensive Look at the Risks and Benefits of MDMA. Rochester, VT, Park Street Press.

Holmes, D.S. (1987) The influence of meditation versus rest on physiological arousal. In M. West (ed.) The Psychology of Meditation. Oxford, Clarendon Press, 81-103.

Holmstrom, David. 1992, Christian Science Monitor

Holt, J. (1999) Blindsight in debates about qualia. Journal of Consciousness Studies 6(5), 54-71.

Holloway RL (1996) Evolution of the human brain. In: Lock A, Peters CR (eds) Handbook of human symbolic evolution. Oxford University Press, Oxford

Iacoboni M, Woods RP, Brass M, Bekkering H, Mazziotta JC, Rizzolatti G (1999) Cortical mechanisms of human imitation. Science 286: 2526–2528.

Iacoboni M, Koski LM, Brass M, Bekkering H, Woods RP, Dubeau MC, Mazziotta JC, Rizzolatti G (2001) Reafferent copies of imitated actions in the right superior temporal cortex. Proc Natl Acad Sci USA 98: 13995–13999.

Jeannerod M (1988) The neural and behavioural organization of goal-directed movements. Clarendon Press, Oxford.

Johnson-Frey SH, Maloof FR, Newman-Norlund R, Farrer C, Inati S, Grafton ST (2003) Actions or hand-objects interactions? Human inferior frontal cortex and action observation. Neuron 39: 1053–1058.

Jackson, F. (1982) Epiphenomenal qualia. Philosophical Quarterly 32, 127-36.

James, W. (1890) The Principles of Psychology (2 volumes). London, Macmillan.

James, W. (1902) The Varieties of Religious Experience: A Study in Human Nature. New York and London, Longmans, Green and Co.

Jansen, K. (2001) Ketamine: Dreams and Realities. Sarasota, FL, Multidisciplinary Association for Psychedelic Studies.

Jay, M. (ed.) (1999) Artificial Paradises: A Drugs Reader. London, Penguin.

Jaynes, J. (1976) The Origin of Consciousness in the Breakdown of the Bicameral Mind. New York, Houghton Mifflin.

Johnson, M.K. and Raye, C.L. (1981) Reality monitoring. Psychological Review 88, 67-85.

Kadim I, Mahgoub O, Baqir S et al. (2015) Cultured meat from muscle stem cells: a review of challenges and prospects. J Integr Agr 14: 222–233

Kandel, E. R. In Search of Memory: The Emergence of a New Science of Mind, W. W. Norton & Company (2007).

Kandel E. R. Schwartz JH, Jessel TM. Principles of neural sciences. New York; McGraw Hill, 2000.

Kanwisher, N. (2001) Neural events and perceptual awareness. Cognition

79, 89-113; also reprinted inS. Dehaene (ed.) The Cognitive Neuroscience of Consciousness. Cambridge, MA, MIT Press, 89-113.

Karn, K. and Hayhoe, M. (2000) Memory representations guide targeting eye movements in a natural task. Visual Cognition 7, 673-703.

Kennedy, H., & Dehay, C. (1988). Functional implications of the anatomical organization of the callosal projections of visual areas V1 and V2 in the macaque monkey. Behav. Brain Res., 29, 225–236.

Kentridge, R.W. and Heywood, C.A. (1999) The status of blindsight. Journal of Consciousness Studies 6(5), 3-11.

Kihlstrom, J.F. (1996) Perception without awareness of what is perceived, learning without awareness of what is learned. In M. Velmans (ed.) The Science of Consciousness. London, Routledge, 23-46.

Kosslyn, S.M. (1980) Image and Mind. Cambridge, MA, Harvard University Press.

Kosslyn, S.M. (1988) Aspects of a cognitive neuroscience of mental imagery. Science 240, 1621-6.

Kinsbourne, M. (1995), 'The intralaminar thalamic nucleii', Consciousness and Cognition, 4.

Kjaer, Troels, Camilla Bertelsen, Paola Piccini, David Brooks, Jorgen Alving, and Hans Lou. "Increased Dopamine Tone during Meditation- Induced Change of Consciousness." Cognitive Brain Research 13, no. 2 (April 2002)

Kölmel HW. 1985. Complex visual hallucinations in the hemianopic field. J Neurol Neurosurg Psychiatry.

Koenig, Harold. "Research on Religion, Spirituality, and Mental Health: A Review." Canadian Journal of Psychiatry 54, no. 5 (May 2009)

Koenig, Harold, ed. Handbook of Religion and Mental Health. San Diego, CA: Academic Press, 1998

Kraepelin E. Psychiatry: A Textbook for Students and Physicians. New York, NY: Science History Publications; 1990.

Lauglin, Charles, John McManus, and Eugene d'Aquili. Brain, Symbol, and Experience. 2nd ed. New York: Columbia University Press, 1992

Lakoff, G. and M. Johnson (1999). Philosophy in the flesh. Basic Books: New York.

LeDoux, J. E. (1996). The emotional brain. New York: Simon & Schuster.

LeDoux, J.E. (1992), 'Emotion and the amygdala', in The Amygdala: Neurobiological Aspects of Emo- tion, Memory and Mental Dysfunction, ed J.P. Aggleton (New York: Wiley-Liss).

Levin, D.T. and Simons, D.J. (1997) Failure to detect changes to attended objects in motion pictures. Psychonomic Bulletin and Review 4, 501-6.

Levine,J. (1983) Materialism and qualia: the explanatory gap. Pacific Philosophical Quarterly 64, 354-61.

Levine,J. (2001) Purple Haze: The Puzzle of Consciousness. New York, Oxford University Press. Levine, S. (1979) A Gradual Awakening. New York, Doubleday.

Levinson, B.W. (1965) States of awareness during general anaesthesia. British Journal of Anaesthesia 37, 544-6.

Lewicki, P., Czyzewska, M. and Hoffman, H. (1987) Unconscious acquisition of complex procedural knowledge. Journal of Experimental Psychology: Learning, Memory and Cognition 13, 523-30.

Lewicki, P., Hill, T. and Bizot, E. (1988) Acquisition of procedural knowledge about a pattern of stimuli that cannot be articulated. Cognitive Psychology 20, 24-37.

Lewicki, P., Hill, T. and Czyzewska, M. (1992) Nonconscious acquisition of information. American Psychologist 47, 796-801.

Manthey S, Schubotz RI, von Cramon DY (2003). Premotor cortex in observing erroneous action: an fMRI study. Brain Res Cogn Brain Res 15: 296–307.

Mesulam MM, Mufson EJ (1982) Insula of the old world monkey. III: Efferent cortical output and comments on function. J Comp Neurol 212: 38–52.

Naskar, Abhijit. "Homo: A Brief History of Consciousness", 2015

Naskar, Abhijit. "What is Mind?", 2016

Naskar, Abhijit. "Love, God & Neurons: Memoir of A Scientist who found himself by getting lost", 2016

Naskar, Abhijit. "Principia Humanitas", 2017

Naskar, Abhijit. "We Are All Black: A Treatise on Racism", 2017

Naskar, Abhijit. "Either Civilized or Phobic: A Treatise on Homosexuality", 2017

Naskar, Abhijit. "The Bengal Tigress: A Treatise on Gender Equality", 2017

Naskar, Abhijit. "Morality Absolute", 2017

Naskar, Abhijit. "Build Bridges not Walls: In the name of Americana", 2018

Naskar, Abhijit. "Fabric of Humanity", 2018

Naskar, Abhijit. "Citizens of Peace: Beyond the Savagery of Sovereignty", 2019

Naskar, Abhijit. "The Constitution of The United Peoples of Earth", 2019

Naskar, Abhijit. "Neurons Giveth, Neurons Taketh Away | Abhijit Naskar | TEDxIIMRanchi", 2019 https://www.youtube.com/watch?v=BNX-Q0ySm80

Naskar, Abhijit. "Mission Reality", 2019

Naskar, Abhijit. "Operation Justice: To Make A Society That Needs No Law", 2019

Naskar, Abhijit. "Every Generation Needs Caretakers: The Gospel of Patriotism", 2020

Naskar, Abhijit. "Hurricane Humans: Give me accountability, I'll give you peace", 2020

Naskar, Abhijit. "Revolution Indomable", 2020

Naskar, Abhijit. "Servitude is Sanctitude", 2020

Naskar, Abhijit. "Good Scientist: When Science and Service Combine", 2020

Newberg, Andrew, and Jeremy Iversen. "The Neural Basis of the Complex Mental Task of Meditation: Neurotransmitter and Neurochemical Considerations." Medical Hypotheses 61, no. 2 (2003).

Newberg, Andrew. "How God Changes Your Brain: An Introduction to Jewish Neurotheology", CCAR Journal: The Reform Jewish Quarterly, Winter 2016.

Newberg, Andrew, and Stephanie Newberg. "A Neuropsychological Perspective on Spiritual Development." In Handbook of Spiritual Development in Childhood and Adolescence, edited by Eugene

Roehlkepartain, Pamela King, Linda Wagener, and Peter Benson. London: Sage Publications, Inc., 2005

Newberg, Andrew. "The Neurotheology Link An Intersection Between Spirituality and Health", Alternative and Complimentary Therapies, Vol 21 No 1, February 2015.

Newberg, Andrew, Nancy Wintering, Dharma Khalsa, Hannah Roggenkamp, and Mark Waldman. "Meditation Effects on Cognitive Function and Cerebral Blood Flow in Subjects with Memory Loss: A Preliminary Study." Journal of Alzheimer's Disease 20, no. 2 (2010)

Nash, M. (1995), 'Glimpses of the mind', Time.

Nesse RM. Proximate and evolutionary studies of anxiety, stress and depression: synergy at the interface. Neurosci Biobehav Rev. 1999;23:895-903.

Nicolelis, Miguel. (2011) "Beyond Boundaries: The New Neuroscience of Connecting Brains with Machines---and How It Will Change Our Lives", Times Books

O'Hara, K. and Scutt, T. (1996) There is no hard problem of consciousness. Journal of Consciousness Studies 3(4), 290-302, reprinted in J. Shear (ed.) (1997) Explaining Consciousness. Cambridge, MA, MIT Press, 69-82.

O'Regan, J.K. (1992) Solving the "real" mysteries of visual perception: the world as an outside memory. Canadian Journal of Psychology 46, 461-88.

O'Regan, J.K. and Noe, A. (2001) A sensorimotor account of vision and visual consciousness. Behavioral and Brain Sciences 24(5), 883-917.

O'Regan, J.K., Rensink, R.A. and Clark,].]. (1999) Change-blindness as a result of "mudsplashes." Nature 398, 34.

Ornstein, R.E. (1977) The Psychology of Consciousness (2nd edn). New York, Harcourt.

Ornstein, R.E. (1986) The Psychology of Consciousness (3rd edn). New York, Pehguin.

Ornstein, R.E. (1992) The Evolution of Consciousness. New York, Touchstone.

Penfield W, Faulk ME (1955) The insula: further observations on its function. Brain 78: 445– 470.

Penrose, R. (1994), Shadows of the Mind (Oxford: Oxford University Press).

Penrose, R. (1989), The Emperor's New Mind: Concerning Computers, Minds and The Laws of Physics (Oxford: Oxford University Press).

Persinger, "'I would kill in God's name' role of sex, weekly church attendance, report of a religious experience and limbic lability" Perceptual and Motor Skills 1997.

Persinger "Experimental simulation of the God experience" Neurotheology 2003.

Persinger, Corradini, Clement, Keaney, et al "Neurotheology and its convergence with neuroquantology" NeuroQuantology 2010.

Persinger, Koren and St-Pierre "The electromagnetic induction of mystical and altered states within the laboratory" Journal of Consciousness Exploration and Research 2010.

Persinger "Case report: A prototypical spontaneous 'sensed presence' of a sentient being and concomitant electroencephalographic activity in the clinical laboratory" Neurocase 2008.

Persinger and Saroka "Potential production of Hughlings Jackson's "parasitic consciousness" by physiologically-patterned weak transcerebral magnetic fields: QEEG and source localization" Epilepsy & Behavior 28 (2013).

Persinger. "The neuropsychiatry of paranormal experiences". J Neuropsychiatry Clin Neurosci 2001.

Persinger. "Neuropsychological bases of god beliefs", New York: Praeger, 1987

Persinger. "Temporal lobe epileptic signs and correlative behaviors displayed by normal populations", Journal of General Psychology, 1986

Perry BD, Pollard R. Homeostasis, stress, trauma, and adaptation. A neurodevelopmental view of childhood trauma. Child Adolesc Psychiatr Clin N Am. 1998;7:33.

Paré, D. & Llinás, R. (1995), 'Conscious and preconscious processes as seen from the standpoint of sleep-waking cycle neurophysiology', Neuropsychologia, 33.

Phillips ML, Young AW, Senior C, Brammer M, Andrew C, Calder AJ, Bullmore ET, Perrett DI, Rowland D, Williams SC, Gray JA, David AS (1997) A specific neural substrate for perceiving facial expressions of disgust. Nature 389: 495–498.

Phillips ML, Young AW, Scott SK, Calder AJ, Andrew C, Giampietro V, Williams SC, Bullmore ET, Brammer M, Gray JA (1998) Neural responses to facial and vocal expressions of fear and disgust. Proc R Soc Lond B Biol Sci 265: 1809–1817.

Puce A, Perrett D (2003) Electrophysiological and brain imaging of biological motion. Philosoph Trans Royal Soc Lond, Series B, 358: 435–445.

Ramachandran VS. Behavioral and magnetoencephalographic correlates of plasticity in the adult human brain. Proc Natl Acad Sci USA 1993; 90: 10413–20.

Ramachandran VS. Phantom limbs, neglect syndromes, repressed memories, and Freudian psychology. Int Rev Neurobiol 1994; 37: 291–333.

Ramachandran VS. Plasticity and functional recovery in neurology. Clin Med 2005; 5: 368–73.

Ramachandran VS, Hirstein W. The perception of phantom limbs. The D. O. Hebb lecture. Brain 1998; 121: 1603–30.

Ramachandran VS, Rogers-Ramachandran D, Cobb S. Touching the phantom limb. Nature 1995; 377: 489–90.

Ramachandran VS, Rogers-Ramachandran D. Phantom limbs and

neural plasticity. Arch Neurol 2000; 57: 317–20.

Ramachandran VS, Rogers-Ramachandran D. It's all done with mirrors. Sci Am Mind 2007; 18: 16–9.

Ramachandran VS, Rogers-Ramachandran D. Sensations referred to a patient's phantom arm from another subjects intact arm: perceptual correlates of mirror neurons. Med Hypotheses 2008; 70: 1233–4.

Ramachandran VS, Rogers-Ramachandran D, Stewart M. Perceptual correlates of massive cortical reorganization. Science 1992; 258: 1159–60.

Rizzolatti G, Craighero L (2004) The mirror-neuron system. Annu Rev Neurosci 27: 169–192.

Rizzolatti G, Fogassi L, Gallese V (2001) Neurophysiological mechanisms underlying the understanding and imitation of action. Nature Rev Neurosci 2:661–670.

Rock I, Victor J. Vision and touch: an experimentally created conflict between the two senses. Science 1964; 143: 594–6.

Rose'n B, Lundborg G. Training with a mirror in rehabilitation of the hand. Scand J Plast Reconstr Surg Hand Surg 2005; 39: 104–8.

Roberts, TA; Smalley, J; Ahrendt, D (December 2020). "Effect of gender affirming hormones on athletic performance in transwomen and transmen: implications for sporting organisations and legislators". British Journal of Sports Medicine. 55 (11): 577–583

Royet JP, Plailly J, Delon-Martin C, Kareken DA, Segebarth C (2003) fMRI of emotional responses to odors: influence of hedonic valence and judgment, handedness, and gender. Neuroimage 20: 713–728.

Rozin R Haidt J and McCauley CR (2000) Disgust. In: Lewis M, Haviland-Jones JM (eds) Handbook of Emotion. 2nd Edition. Guilford Press, New York, pp 637–653.

Saxe R, Carey S, Kanwisher N (2004) Understanding other minds: linking developmental psychology and functional neuroimaging. Annu Rev Psychol 55: 87–124.

S. J. Russell and P. Norvig, Artificial intelligence: a modern approach (3rd edition): Prentice Hall, 2009.

Singer T, Seymour B, O'Doherty J, Kaube H, Dolan RJ, Frith CD (2004) Empathy for pain involves the affective but not the sensory components of pain. Science 303: 1157–1162.

Smith A (1759) The theory of moral sentiments (ed. 1976). Clarendon Press, Oxford.

Schilling, Vincent. 2017, indian country today

Stein, Stephen K. 2017, The Sea in World History: Exploration, Travel, and Trade

Simonsen R (2015) Eating for the future: veganism and the challenge of in vitro meat. In: Stapleton P, Byers A (Hg). Biopolitics and utopia. Palgrave Macmillan, New York (2015), S 167–190

Tesla N. "My Inventions", 1919

T. R. Society, "Machine learning: the power and promise of computers that learn by example," ed. The Royal Society, 2017.

Tomasello M, Call J (1997) Primate cognition. Oxford University Press, Oxford.

207